Essential
Casserole Recipes

Barbara C. Jones

Main Street
A division of Sterling Publishing Co., Inc.
New York

Library of Congress Cataloging-in-Publication Data Available

10 9 8 7 6 5 4 3 2 1

Published by Sterling Publishing Co., Inc.

387 Park Avenue South, New York, NY 10016

© 2005 by Sterling Publishing

Designed by Liz Trovato

Photography by Evan Bracken, Light Reflections

This book is comprised of materials from the Sterling title *The Ultimate Casserole Cookbook*
© 2002 by Barbara C. Jones

Distributed in Canada by Sterling Publishing

c/o Canadian Manda Group, 165 Dufferin Street

Toronto, Ontario, Canada M6K 3H6

Distributed in Great Britain by Chrysalis Books Group PLC

The Chrysalis Building, Bramley Road, London W10 6SP, England

Distributed in Australia by Capricorn Link (Australia) Pty. Ltd.

P.O. Box 704, Windsor, NSW 2756, Australia

Printed in China

Sterling ISBN 1-4027-1671-0

Introduction

This cookbook is an eclectic mix of flavors and skill levels. From regional specialties to gourmet delights, the recipes offer delectable taste treats for both the simplest and the most educated of human palates. Such a claim can rarely be made and fulfilled, but with the lowly and the grand casserole, it is possible.

The real beginning of the casserole could have started when man began cooking food in pots and combining more than two ingredients. Its roots go back to every generation and every ethnic background. The casserole survives because of its modern adaptations, but still manages to provoke the emotions of comfort, warmth, and security. It survives today as a practical family meal or an elaborate gourmet event. The scope and depth of this simple yet imperial dish can be found in the pages of *Essential Casserole Recipes.*

In its modest beginnings, the casserole referred to a pan or pot with a lid in which food was cooked. When several ingredients were cooked in the casserole pot or pan, the food itself became known as a casserole. And so today, the word "casserole" means both the container and the food it serves.

Casserole containers themselves started out as large, heavy iron pots with lids, handles, and feet for cooking over open fires. Lids kept the heat in and provided a moist cooking environment that made even the poorest cuts of meat tender if cooked long enough. To this day, characteristics such as lids and handles have survived because of the practical nature of the casserole itself. The idea of serving food in the same container in which it was cooked has led to elaborate containers and food combinations.

Casserole containers come in many sizes, shapes, and materials. The Dutch oven is the oldest of containers still in use. It's a large kettle or pot, favored in cast iron, usually with an opening larger than its base, with a tight fitting lid and handles.

Today's casserole dishes are round, oval, square, and rectangular, and they're able to hold varying amounts. They can be shallow or deep, or any depth in between. They can be made of copper, cast iron, enameled iron, stainless steel, aluminum, ceramic, or glass. Their size, shape, and material become the cook's choice as do the foods prepared in them.

The casserole's convenience, practicality, elegance, and simplicity all work to give us one of the most popular and versatile of all food combinations . . . and it even comes with its own container.

Enjoy and celebrate!

Casserole Basics

Casseroles can generally be defined as one-dish meals combining more than two or three ingredients, cooked in the oven, and served in the same dish in which they were cooked. They can be baked in containers in a wide variety of sizes, shapes, and materials.

Basic Pan Materials

When choosing casseroles or baking dishes, the heaviest is usually the best. The heaviest-gauge pans spread and hold heat evenly, thereby cooking the contents without burning. They also will last longer and have a tendency not to warp. Also, lids with casseroles are very helpful. Glass casseroles or baking dishes may be covered with aluminum foil for the oven and plastic wrap for the refrigerator, but lids are preferable with other materials. Listed below are materials, sizes, and shapes for various casseroles, baking dishes, and pans. Beyond the basics mentioned, personal preference as to looks and how you plan to use the pans should guide your buying decisions.

Cast Iron

Some cooks believe a cast-iron skillet is a must in the kitchen to get the "old-fashioned" flavors they remember from mother or grandmother. Cast iron is a very good material for cooking because it cooks food evenly, and it can go from the stovetop to the oven. The problem comes when you move it from the stovetop to the oven and then take it out of the oven, because it can be very heavy. That may not seem like much of a problem, but wait until you have a cast-iron pot, skillet, or sauté pan full of steaming, hot food and you're gripping it with two hands, carrying it from one place to another. That's when reality sets in and "heavy" takes on a new meaning.

Copper

Copper is the chef's delight but is usually left to the professionals because of the expense. Besides looking great and cooking food evenly, it's undeniably the best type of pan. It's great if you can afford it.

Coated Aluminum

Heavy-duty aluminum with nonstick coatings (which eventually do wear out regardless of the manufacturer's claims) are very popular because they are reasonably priced, lighter weight, and cook food evenly. Those that are anodized are stronger and will probably last longer.

Stainless Steel

Stainless steel is one step up from anodized aluminum in appearance. If anodized aluminum or heavy-duty aluminum with nonstick surfaces isn't good-looking enough for you, and copper is out of your price range, check out stainless steel. All good stainless steel pans have a layer of copper or aluminum on the bottom and sides or a layer sandwiched between the coatings of stainless steel. Make sure they are heavy and not lightweight.

Enameled Iron

Enameled iron puts a pretty face on a plain pan. The more expensive ones have the qualities needed for cooking with the outside attractiveness needed for the dinner table. Don't let the outside distract you from the material properties, however. When your casserole dish is sitting on the table looking great for honored dinner guests, you want its contents to taste as good as the pan looks.

Ceramic

Ceramic- or porcelain-coated metal falls into the same category as enameled iron. It was created for its attractiveness at the table. Just make sure the metal's properties meet your needs.

Glass

Glass pans are probably the most inexpensive and widely used. It's the type of dish you use for most family meals. It's also the dish you take to potluck suppers. If it gets broken or lost during the cleanup, you won't be devastated. You'll just go buy another one, tape your name to the bottom, and take it to the next potluck supper.

Pan Sizes

If you could choose only three size pans, you might consider the 8- x 12-inch rectangular pan, the 9- x 13-inch rectangular pan, and the 9-inch square pan. If you could just have one, the 9- x 13-inch would have to be the first choice. Its general all-purpose size and shape holds most of the casseroles found in this book. But don't take our word for it, shop around and check out all the sizes and shapes available—you won't believe the variety.

Casserole Containers

7 x 11 x 2 yields 6 to 8 cups
9 x 9 x 2 yields 10 cups
9 x 13 x 2 yields 15 cups

Sauce Pans

Small: 1 to 2 cups
Medium: 6 cups (1 1/2 quarts, 1.65 L)
Large: 16 cups (4 quarts, 4.4 L)
Note: It's important for all pots and pans to have lids.

Pasta Pans

4- to 8-quart (4.4 to 8.8 L) pot large enough for 1 to 2 pounds (454 to 908 g) of pasta and its equivalent water.

Freezing Casseroles

Baking and freezing casseroles can be a great way to save time and money. For best success, follow the guidelines below.

1. Cook casserole as directed, but reduce cooking time by 10 to 15 minutes so it won't overcook when it's reheated.
2. Always cover casserole or baking dishes tightly before freezing.
3. Use an oven-to-freezer container so you don't have to disturb the dish before freezing.
4. Reduce the amounts of seasonings used because they may intensify with time.
5. Let casserole cool before freezing.
6. Store in freezer no more than 2 to 4 weeks.
7. Defrost food in refrigerator.

Chicken Tetrazzini

Prep time: 15 minutes • **Cooking time: 30–45 minutes** • **Makes 6 servings** • **Calories: 1,090, Carbs: 74g, Protein: 72g, Fat: 55g**

A different tetrazzini—thick, creamy, and full of flavor!

5 quarts (5 L) water

3 pounds (1.4 kg) boneless, skinless chicken breast halves

3 bacon slices, halved

2 ribs celery, chopped

2 tablespoons Creole seasoning

1 tablespoon salt

1/2 teaspoon garlic powder

1/4 teaspoon pepper

2 10 1/2-ounce (297 g) cans chicken broth (optional)

1 pound (453 g) package thin spaghetti

1 pound (453 g) fresh mushrooms, stemmed

2 to 4 cloves garlic, minced

2 to 4 tablespoons butter

3/4 cup (170 g) butter, melted

3/4 cup (105 g) flour

1/2 pint (240 mL) whipping cream

1 1/2 cups (130 g) grated parmesan cheese, divided

Pour water into large pot and add chicken, bacon, celery, Creole seasoning, and salt. Bring to a boil, cover, and simmer for about 1 1/2 hours.

Reserve broth and cut chicken into bite-sized pieces. Bring broth to a boil and add spaghetti. Cook until slightly tender. Drain spaghetti into separate bowl to reserve broth and set aside.

Measure remaining broth and pour into stock pot. There should be 8 to 10 cups (1.9 to 2.4 L) broth. If not, add cans of chicken broth to equal this amount. Bring broth to boil, then simmer until broth is reduced to 5 cups (1.2 L).

Sauté whole mushrooms and garlic in butter and set aside. In saucepan, melt 3/4 cup butter and stir in flour. Gradually add broth, stirring constantly, until thickened. Add cream and cook until it's a thick and creamy sauce.

In 3 1/2-quart (3 L) baking dish, layer half the spaghetti, half the chicken, half the mushrooms, and half the cheese. Pour half the cream sauce over mixture.

Repeat layers with remaining spaghetti, chicken, and mushrooms, and top with parmesan. Bake at 350° (175° C) for 30 to 45 minutes.

Chicken Avocado Casserole

Prep time: 15 minutes • **Cooking time: 1 hour, 10 minutes** • **Makes 6 servings** • **Calories: 547, Carbs: 20g, Protein: 32g, Fat: 36g**

The outstanding avocado perks up many a dish, and with chicken, this dish is tops.

1/4 cup (35g) flour

Salt and pepper to taste

1/4 teaspoon thyme

6 boneless, skinless chicken breast halves

8 tablespoons (115g) butter, divided

1 small onion, chopped

1 cup (240 mL) dry white wine

2/3 cup (160 mL) chicken broth

1 chicken bouillon cube

1 1/2 tablespoons flour

2/3 cup (160 mL) cream

3 avocados

Lemon juice

Oil

In a bowl mix together flour, salt, pepper, and thyme. Roll chicken in mixture. In a skillet, melt 5 tablespoons butter and brown chicken. Place in sprayed baking dish.

Add remaining butter to skillet and brown onions. Add wine, chicken broth, and bouillon blended with flour. Bring to a boil and cook until thick. Pour mixture over chicken.

Cover and cook at 375° (190° C) for 1 hour. Remove from oven. Cool slightly and stir in cream. Sprinkle peeled, sliced avocados with lemon juice. Place on chicken and brush with small amount of oil. Return to oven for 10 minutes.

South American Chicken

Prep time: 5 minutes • **Cooking time: 20–25 minutes** • **Makes 4 servings** • **Calories: 733, Carbs: 5g, Protein: 60g, Fat: 53g**

This is like having a chicken fiesta for dinner.

4 boneless, skinless chicken breasts
1 14-ounce (396g) can hearts of palm, drained
Melted butter
½ teaspoon salt
¼ teaspoon white pepper
3 egg whites
1 tablespoon lemon juice
½ teaspoon salt
¼ teaspoon pepper
1 cup (230g) butter, melted
Fresh parsley
Hungarian paprika

Flatten chicken breasts slightly with a meat tenderizer. Wrap each one around a stalk of hearts of palm. Brush with melted butter and season with salt and pepper.

Bake, uncovered, at 400° (200° C) for 20 to 25 minutes, basting several times with drippings. Place egg whites, lemon juice, salt, and pepper in a blender.

With motor on, slowly drip hot melted butter into blender to make a good emulsion. Garnish chicken with parsley and paprika and pour sauce over chicken. Serve.

Chardonnay Chicken

Prep time: 20 minutes (refrigerate overnight) • **Cooking time: 40 minutes** • **Makes 6 to 8 servings** • **Calories: 666, Carbs: 40g, Protein: 54g, Fat: 32g**

Invite the new neighbors over, and you'll have friends for life.

3 onions, sliced thinly, divided

1 bell pepper, chopped

2 cloves garlic, minced

  Butter

7 to 8 boneless, skinless chicken breast halves

  Salt

  Pepper

  Garlic powder

1 14-ounce (396g) can artichoke hearts, halved, drained

2 1/4 cups (200g) grated gruyere cheese

2 cups (180g) breadcrumbs

1 tablespoon tarragon

1/4 cup (60g) butter, melted

1 bottle Chardonnay wine

Sauté onion, bell pepper, and garlic in butter until tender and translucent. Spoon two-thirds of mixture into sprayed 9- x 13-inch (23 x 33 cm) baking dish and spread over bottom of dish.

Sprinkle both sides of chicken pieces with salt, pepper, and a little garlic powder and place over onion–bell pepper mixture. Scatter artichoke hearts over chicken, then add remaining onion mixture.

In a separate bowl, mix together cheese, breadcrumbs, tarragon, and melted butter and pour over chicken. Pour wine into dish to cover chicken halfway. Cover baking dish and refrigerate overnight.

To prepare, bake at 350° (175° C) for 20 minutes; remove cover and bake another 20 minutes until bubbly and golden brown on top. Don't overcook.

Mushroom Chicken Stroganoff

Prep time: 20 minutes • **Cooking time: 30 minutes** • **Makes 4 servings** • **Calories: 589, Carbs: 11g, Protein: 59g, Fat: 32g**

A new twist on stroganoff!

8 boneless, skinless chicken breast halves

Salt

Pepper

1/2 cup (115g) butter

2 onions, quartered

1/2 pound (226g) mushrooms, stemmed, chopped

1 tablespoon flour

1/2 cup (120 mL) chicken broth

1/2 cup (120 mL) dry white wine

1/2 cup (120g) sour cream

3 tablespoons dijon mustard

Cooked rice

Parsley

Season both sides of chicken with salt and pepper and cut into bite-sized pieces. Sauté in skillet with half the butter until lightly brown on outside.

Simmer about 5 to 10 minutes more until opaque, stirring occasionally. Remove chicken from heat, and set aside in baking dish with lid on to keep warm.

Sauté onions and mushrooms until tender and translucent. Pour into chicken mixture and cover with lid. Melt remaining butter in skillet and add flour, stirring continuously for about 3 minutes to remove lumps. Whisk in broth and wine, stirring constantly to thicken sauce.

Cook for about 5 minutes, then add sour cream and mustard. Simmer for another 5 minutes and stir occasionally to mix and heat throughout. Pour over chicken and warm in oven about 5 to 10 minutes. Serve over rice and garnish with parsley.

Chicken Enchiladas Olé

Prep time: 10 minutes • **Cooking time: 20–25 minutes** • **Makes 4 servings** • **Calories: 754, Carbs: 38g, Protein: 55g, Fat: 43g**

You will look forward to these enchiladas all day long!

  4 boneless, skinless chicken breast halves
  1 bunch green onions, tops only
 10 peppercorns
  3 ribs celery
 ½ teaspoon salt
 13 ounce (368g) can tomatillos, drained
  4 ounce (113g) can chopped green chilies
 ⅓ cup (20g) cilantro leaves, snipped
 ¾ cup (180 mL) whipping cream
  2 eggs
 ¼ cup (45g) chopped pickled jalapeños, seeded (optional)
  2 cups (110g) shredded Monterey Jack cheese, divided
 ½ cup (40g) grated fresh parmesan cheese
 ½ teaspoon salt
 ½ teaspoon white pepper
    Olive oil
  8 corn tortillas

In large saucepan, combine chicken, chopped onion tops, peppercorns, celery, and salt, and cover with water. Bring to a boil, reduce heat, and cook on low until chicken is tender. Drain and let chicken cool.

Combine tomatillos, green chilies, cilantro, whipping cream, and eggs in blender, and process until smooth. Set aside.

Chop chicken and mix with chopped green onions, jalapeños, 1 cup Monterey Jack cheese, and parmesan in a bowl. Season with salt and white pepper. Heat oil in skillet and cook tortilla until soft. Remove from skillet and drain.

Lay tortilla flat and spoon one-eighth of chicken mixture into center. Form chicken into compact shape and roll tortilla up tightly. Place filled tortilla, seam side down, in sprayed 9- x 13-inch (23 x 33 cm) baking dish.

Repeat with remaining 7 tortillas and pour tomatillo mixture evenly over tortillas. Sprinkle remaining Monterey Jack cheese over top. Bake at 350° (175° C) for 20 to 25 minutes until bubbly.

Quail à l'Orange

Prep time: 25 minutes • **Cooking time: 1 hour, 15 minutes** • **Makes 8 servings** • **Calories: 384, Carbs: 9g, Protein: 23g, Fat: 27g**

Oranges add a zesty citrus flavor to this classic quail recipe, and their bright color looks nice in the finished dish.

1	teaspoon seasoned salt
½	cup (70g) flour
¼	teaspoon pepper
8	quail, dressed
½	cup (120 mL) oil
½	onion, chopped
½	green bell pepper, chopped
1	clove garlic, minced
1	carrot, sliced
1	cup (240 mL) chicken broth
1	cup (240 mL) white wine
1	tablespoon grated orange rind
1	teaspoon Worcestershire sauce
	Sour cream at room temperature

Mix salt, flour, and pepper in a paper bag. Put quail in bag and shake until lightly coated. In skillet, heat oil and quickly brown quail over medium-high heat. Put quail in sprayed baking dish.

Sauté onion, bell pepper, and garlic in remaining oil. Add carrot, broth, and wine. Cover and simmer for 15 minutes. Pour over quail and sprinkle with orange rind and Worcestershire sauce.

Cover and bake at 350° (175° C) for 45 minutes. Turn off heat and leave in oven an additional 30 minutes. Serve with a dab of sour cream.

Beef Stew Casserole

Prep time: 10 minutes • Cooking time: 5 hours • Makes 4 servings • Calories: 590, Carbs: 28g, Protein: 54g, Fat: 28g

This recipe is so easy—you spend just 10 minutes putting it together, and then you have five hours of blissful relaxation while the oven does all the work for you!

- 2 pounds (907g) stew meat, cut in bite-sized pieces
- 1 cup (150g) sliced carrots
- 1 onion, chopped
- 4 potatoes, peeled, cubed
- 1 cup (100g) chopped celery
- 2 teaspoons salt
- 1 teaspoon pepper
- 1 10 ½ ounce (297g) can cream of mushroom soup
- ½ cup (120 mL) water
- 1 dried bay leaf, crumbled
- ½ cup (120 mL) burgundy wine

Mix all ingredients in a sprayed baking dish. Bake at 275° (135° C) for 5 hours.

Lamb and Eggplant Casserole

Prep time: 15 minutes • **Cooking time: 30–40 minutes** • **Makes 4 servings** • **Calories: 361, Carbs: 10g, Protein: 21g, Fat: 27g**

Lamb and eggplant make for a nice change of pace from chicken and beef!

 1 pound (453g) ground lamb

 1 large eggplant

 1 large tomato, chopped

 ½ cup (75g) chopped green onions with tops

1½ teaspoons salt

 ½ teaspoon curry powder

 ½ teaspoon paprika

 4 tablespoons snipped parsley

Brown ground lamb in skillet, drain on paper towels, and set aside to cool. Peel and finely chop one eggplant.

Combine lamb, eggplant, tomato, onions, salt, curry powder, paprika, and parsley and stir to mix thoroughly.

Spoon the mixture into a sprayed baking dish and spread evenly. Bake at 350° (175° C) for 30 to 40 minutes until top is brown.

Stromboli Hero

Prep time: 15 minutes • Cooking time: 10–15 minutes • Makes 4 servings • Calories: 1,029, Carbs: 30g, Protein: 52g, Fat: 77g

News flash! A loaf of bread filled with meat and cheese—what more could you ask for?

3/4 pound (340g) ground beef

Salt

Pepper

1 pound (453g) ground pork sausage

1/4 teaspoon salt

1/4 teaspoon pepper

1/2 teaspoon rosemary

2 cloves garlic, minced

1/2 cup (40g) grated parmesan cheese

1 15 ounce (425g) can tomato sauce

1 loaf French bread

8 ounce (226g) package mozzarella cheese

Season ground beef with salt and pepper. Brown in skillet with pork sausage until brown and crumbly. Stir in rosemary, garlic, parmesan, and tomato sauce, and simmer to reduce liquid.

Cut top off French bread in horizontal slice and hollow out bread from inside, leaving crust of 1/4 to 1/2 inch (.5 to 1 cm) shell. Sprinkle half the mozzarella in shell, then all of the meat mixture, and then the remaining mozzarella.

Replace horizontal top on bread shell. Wrap in foil and place in a 9- x 13-inch (23 x 33 cm) baking dish. Bake at 350° (175° C) for 10 to 15 minutes or until heated thoroughly.

Moussaka

Prep time: 45 minutes • **Cooking time: 45 minutes** • **Makes 6 servings** • **Calories: 900, Carbs: 48g, Protein: 45g, Fat: 59g**

This is an old-time Greek recipe and takes a little more preparation, but it's well worth it.

1/2 cup (120 mL) olive oil, divided

3 cloves garlic, minced

1 onion, chopped

1 1/2 pounds (680g) ground round or chuck

2 teaspoons basil

1 teaspoon oregano

1/2 teaspoon cinnamon

1/2 teaspoon seasoned salt

1/2 teaspoon pepper

2 8 ounce (226g) cans tomato sauce

2 pounds (900g) eggplant

Salt

2 baking potatoes

3 eggs

2 tablespoons flour

2 cups (480g) plain yogurt or sour cream

1/2 to 3/4 cup (40 to 60g) grated parmigiano-reggiano cheese

To make meat sauce, heat 2 tablespoons oil in large skillet and sauté garlic and onion until onion is translucent. Add ground meat, brown, and reduce heat to cook until meat is no longer pink. Drain and return to skillet.

Add basil, oregano, cinnamon, seasoned salt, pepper, and tomato sauce. Increase heat to boiling, then reduce heat to low and simmer for 15 minutes, stirring occasionally. Set aside.

To make eggplant mixture, cut eggplant into thick slices, salt both sides, and place in colander. Set aside for 15 to 20 minutes. Peel potatoes and slice thinly. In a saucepan, cover potatoes with water, bring to a boil, and reduce heat to simmer until potatoes are fork tender. Drain and set aside.

After beads of liquid form on the eggplant, use a paper towel to pat dry. Brush with olive oil and place under broiler for 3 to 4 minutes per side or until both sides are golden brown.

To make topping, beat eggs and gradually add flour while beating. Add yogurt and mix thoroughly. Make sure mixture is smooth without any lumps.

Place some of the eggplant and potato slices in one layer on bottom of a sprayed 9- x 13-inch (23 x 33 cm) baking dish. Spoon half the meat mixture evenly over the eggplant and potato slices.

Repeat layers using all the eggplant and potato slices. Spoon yogurt sauce over top and spread to smooth. Sprinkle with cheese and bake at 375° (190° C) for 40 to 45 minutes or until bubbly and golden brown.

Spicy Lasagna

Prep time: 30 minutes • Cooking time: 30–35 minutes • Makes 6 servings • Calories: 882, Carbs: 37g, Protein: 55g, Fat: 58g

Hot sausages mean this recipe has the authority to please.

- 1 pound (453g) hot Italian sausage
- 8 ounce (226g) package hot pork sausage
- 1 onion, chopped
- 3 cloves garlic, minced
- 2 tablespoons oil
- 1 28-ounce (793g) can crushed tomatoes
- 1 6-ounce (170g) can tomato paste
- 1 1/2 teaspoon basil
- 1 1/2 teaspoons oregano
- 1/2 teaspoon salt
- 1 cup (85g) grated parmesan cheese
- 2 cups (480g) small-curd cottage cheese, drained
- 1 egg, beaten
- 1 cup fresh parsley, snipped, divided
- 6 lasagna noodles, cooked
- 1 12-ounce package shredded mozzarella cheese, divided

Brown sausages in large skillet until crumbly and no longer pink. Drain through strainer and remove grease from skillet. Sauté onion and garlic with oil in skillet. Cook until translucent and stir to keep from burning.

Add crushed tomatoes, tomato paste, and seasonings, and stir to mix. Allow to cook until liquid has thickened enough to be spooned out of skillet and spread easily over noodles. Add sausage to the tomato mixture and stir to mix.

In a separate bowl, add parmesan, cottage cheese, egg, and half the parsley. Stir to mix. In a sprayed 9- x 13-inch (23 x 33 cm) baking dish, spoon out a thin layer of sausage-tomato mixture over the bottom of the dish.

Layer half the noodles, half the parmesan mixture, half the mozzarella, and half the sausage-tomato mixture. Repeat the layers using the remaining noodles, parmesan mixture, mozzarella, and sausage-tomato mixture.

Sprinkle the top with remaining parsley. Cover with foil and bake at 350° (175° C) for 30 to 35 minutes until bubbly.

Sweet and Sour Cabbage Rolls

Prep time: 50 minutes • Cooking time: 1 hour 45 minutes • Makes 6 servings • Calories: 638, Carbs: 43g, Protein: 34g, Fat: 38g

This dish tastes wonderful and best of all, it tastes even better on the second day!

¼ cup (60 mL) olive oil

½ cup (75g) minced onion

½ cup (50g) minced celery

4 cloves garlic, minced

2 28-ounce (793g) cans crushed tomatoes

1 tablespoon tomato paste

¼ cup (60 mL) dry red wine

¼ cup (15g) minced fresh parsley

2 tablespoons minced fresh basil

1 tablespoon oregano

½ teaspoon nutmeg

½ to 1 teaspoon salt

½ teaspoon black pepper

¼ teaspoon cayenne

1 head green cabbage

1 15-ounce (425g) can stewed tomatoes

1 cup (240 mL) water

1 tablespoon lemon juice

¼ cup (25g) packed brown sugar

1 teaspoon ground ginger

¾ cup (180g) cooked white rice

8 ounces (226g) ground pork sausage

1 pound (453g) ground chuck roast

½ cup (75g) chopped green onion with tops

½ teaspoon thyme

1 teaspoon caraway seeds

1 teaspoon salt

1 teaspoon pepper

1½ cups (225g) sauerkraut, rinsed, drained, divided
Fresh parsley

In heavy saucepan, heat oil and sauté onion, celery, and garlic. Cook until ingredients are tender and translucent. Over medium heat, pour in tomatoes, tomato paste, red wine, parsley, basil, oregano, nutmeg, salt, pepper, and cayenne. Cook for 10 to 15 minutes, stirring occasionally.

Tear off 8 to 10 large whole cabbage leaves and wash. Fill large pot half full of water and bring to a boil. Submerge cabbage leaves in boiling water, one at a time, and cook for 5 minutes or until tender. Shock leaves in bowl of cold water, then drain and set aside.

To tomato sauce mixture, add stewed tomatoes, water, lemon juice, brown sugar, and ginger. Stir to mix and set aside.

In separate bowl, mix together rice, pork, beef, green onions, thyme, caraway seeds, salt, and pepper. Stir to mix well. In a sprayed baking dish spread 1 cup sauerkraut over bottom.

Spread out several whole cabbage leaves. Fill center with ⅓ to ½ cup of filling. Fold one side over filling, then fold in both ends. Roll tightly to hold ends in place. Place seam side down in baking dish with sauerkraut. Arrange cabbage rolls in one layer on top of sauerkraut, then add remaining sauerkraut.

Bring tomato sauce mixture to a boil and pour over sauerkraut and cabbage rolls. Cover with aluminum foil and bake at 350° (175° C) for 1 hour and 45 minutes. Garnish with fresh parsley and serve.

Creole Chicken and Shrimp

Prep time: 20 minutes • **Cooking time: 40–45 minutes** • **Makes 6 servings** • **Calories: 378, Carbs: 9g, Protein: 44g, Fat: 17g**

The best of the culinary world!

1	tablespoon pickling spice
1 1/2	pounds (680g) shrimp, peeled, veined
4	tablespoons olive oil
4	boneless, skinless chicken breast halves
1	bunch green onions and tops, chopped
1/2	cup (50g) chopped celery
1/3	cup (60g) chopped red bell pepper
1/3	cup (60g) chopped green bell pepper
1	8-ounce (226g) can tomato sauce
1/2	cup (120 mL) white wine
1/4	teaspoon Tabasco sauce
1	tablespoon Worcestershire sauce
2	to 3 tablespoons snipped parsley
1/4	teaspoon thyme
1 1/2	teaspoons salt
1/2	teaspoon pepper
1	cup (240g) half-and-half
	Rice

Fill large pot three-quarters full with water and bring to a boil. Add pickling spice and shrimp and cook until shrimp turn pink. Remove shrimp, drain, and chill.

In large skillet, heat oil and brown chicken on both sides. Sauté until centers are no longer pink. Remove from skillet and drain on paper towels. Cool and cut into bite-sized pieces.

Put onions, celery, and peppers in the skillet and sauté until onion is translucent. Add chicken to skillet and stir in tomato sauce, white wine, Tabasco, Worcestershire sauce, parsley, thyme, salt, and pepper, and mix well.

Pour into a 4-quart (4.5 L) baking dish and bake at 350° (175° C) for 40 to 45 minutes. Remove chicken dish and stir in shrimp and half-and-half. Bake until heated throughout. Serve over rice.

Snow Pea Shrimp

Prep time: 20 minutes • **Cooking time 20–25 minutes** • **Makes 6 servings** • **Calories: 630, Carbs: 55g, Protein: 37g, Fat: 29g**

With pasta, shrimp, snow peas, and cheese, you can't go wrong.

3 cups (300g) penne pasta

1/2 cup (115g) butter

3 cloves garlic, minced

2 green onions, minced

2 cups (150g) sliced fresh mushrooms

1/2 cup (70g) flour

1/2 teaspoon salt

1/2 teaspoon pepper

1 15-ounce (425g) can chicken broth

2 cups (480 mL) milk

3 tablespoons dry white wine

3/4 cup (80g) grated Swiss cheese

2 1/4 cups (250g) frozen snow peas, thawed and drained

1 pound (453g) fresh shrimp, cleaned, cooked, peeled

1/2 cup (40g) grated parmesan cheese

1/4 to 1/2 cup (20 to 40g) sliced almonds

Cook and drain pasta according to package directions. In a large deep skillet, melt butter and sauté garlic, onion, and mushrooms over low heat. Continue cooking until mushrooms are tender; stir occasionally.

Add flour, salt, and pepper, stirring constantly over medium heat. Stir until all lumps are out and sauce is smooth and bubbly. Gradually stir in broth, milk, and wine and stir continuously until smooth.

Turn to high heat, bring to boiling, and stir in Swiss cheese. Stir until cheese is melted and remove from heat. Add snow peas, shrimp, and pasta to mushroom mixture and stir to mix well.

Pour into sprayed 9- x 13-inch (23 x 33 cm) baking dish. Sprinkle parmesan and almonds over top. Bake at 350° (175° C) for 20 to 25 minutes or until golden brown on top.

Seafood Baked Tomatoes

Prep time: 20 minutes • Cooking time: 20 minutes • Makes 6 servings • Calories: 156, Carbs: 11g, Protein: 14g, Fat: 6g

Here's a quick casserole that looks stunning. Feel free to use canned crabmeat or shrimp if you don't have fresh seafood on hand.

6	large, firm tomatoes
	Salt
2	tablespoons butter
4	tablespoons minced green onions and tops
4	tablespoons minced celery
4	tablespoons minced green or red bell pepper
1 1/2	tablespoons flour
1 1/2	cups (360 mL) milk
1 1/2	cups (600g) crabmeat, chopped lobster, or shrimp
2	teaspoons Worcestershire sauce
1/2	teaspoon cayenne pepper
1/2	teaspoon salt
1	cup (100g) grated cheddar cheese
	Lettuce
	Green onions with tops, sliced
	Radishes
	Celery with leaves
	Parsley

Hollow out tomatoes from stem end, leaving enough meat to hold shape of tomato. Hollow out enough area to fill with seafood mixture for one serving. Lightly salt inside of tomatoes and invert on rack to drain for about 15 minutes.

In a skillet, melt butter and sauté onion, celery, and green pepper until tender and translucent. Stir in flour and whisk until smooth and all lumps are removed. Slowly stir in milk, stirring constantly.

Continue cooking and stirring until sauce has thickened to gravy consistency. Add seafood of choice and continue to stir. Add Worcestershire, cayenne, salt, and cheese, and stir until cheese has melted. Remove from heat.

Put tomato shells in baking dish, closed side down, and spoon in filling. Put baking dish in a roasting pan containing several inches of water and place in 350° (175° C) oven for 20 minutes. If tomatoes are ripe and shells don't hold their shape very well, put tomato shells in sprayed or well-buttered muffin tins.

Serve on a bed of lettuce and garnish with green onions, radish slices, celery stalks, and parsley.

Crabmeat Quiche

Prep time: 10 minutes • **Cooking time: 40 minutes** • **Makes 6 servings** • **Calories: 366, Carbs: 20g, Protein: 13g, Fat: 26g**

Whether for lunch or brunch—crabmeat quiche is a winner!

1   6-ounce (170g) can crabmeat, drained

6   to 8 fresh mushrooms, sliced

$^2/_3$ cup (100g) chopped green onion

$^1/_2$ cup (55g) grated Swiss cheese

1   9-inch (23 cm) unbaked pie shell

2   eggs, beaten

$^1/_2$ cup (120 mL) milk

$^1/_2$ cup (120g) mayonnaise

2   tablespoons flour

$^1/_2$ teaspoon salt

$^1/_2$ stick (60g) butter, melted

Flake crabmeat and remove shells. Combine crabmeat, mushrooms, green onion, and cheese, and place in pie shell.

Combine eggs, milk, mayonnaise, flour, and salt, and beat well. Pour slowly over crabmeat. Add melted butter and bake at 350° (175° C) for 40 minutes.

Three-Cheese Fusilli Bake

Prep time: 15 minutes • **Cooking time: 45 minutes** • **Makes 4 servings** • **Calories: 903, Carbs: 62g, Protein: 37g, Fat: 54g**

If you don't have a soufflé dish, a deep, round casserole dish will work fine.

1 tablespoon salt

1 tablespoon olive oil

1 pound (453g) spinach fusilli

1 cup (240 mL) whipping cream

1/2 cup (120 mL) dry white wine

1/2 teaspoon Tabasco

1 1/2 cups (165g) blue cheese

1 cup (110g) brie cheese, rind removed, cubed

3 cups (330g) grated cheddar cheese, divided

1 tablespoon dried thyme

2 tablespoons sage

1 to 2 tablespoons ground white pepper to taste

4 to 5 roma tomatoes, peeled, thinly sliced

3 tablespoons grated parmesan cheese

2 tablespoons snipped fresh basil

Fill a large pot three-quarters full of water and bring to a boil. Add salt, oil, and fusilli, and cook until fusilli is al dente. Drain and rinse under cold water. Repeat process and set aside.

In heavy saucepan, slowly heat to simmering whipping cream, wine, and Tabasco, stirring constantly. Gradually add all cheeses, except 1 cup cheddar, a little at a time as they melt. Whisk or stir constantly as cheese melts and be sure not to let milk scorch or burn on bottom of saucepan.

When cheeses have melted and mixture is smooth and creamy, whisk in thyme, sage, and white pepper. Remove from heat and continue stirring for 3 to 5 minutes as cheese mixture cools.

In a sprayed 2 1/2-quart (2.5 L) soufflé dish, arrange one-third of the cheese mixture over the fusilli and sprinkle one-third of the remaining grated cheddar cheese. Repeat process in two more layers, ending with grated cheddar on top.

Carefully put soufflé dish in oven, bake at 350° (175° C) for 15 to 20 minutes. Remove from oven, cover with aluminum foil, and bake another 15 minutes.

Remove from oven and uncover. Place tomato slices over the top in a nice overlapping design, and sprinkle parmesan on top. Bake at 350° (175° C) for another 10 minutes uncovered. Remove from oven, sprinkle with fresh basil, and serve.

Italian Manicotti

Prep time: 20 minutes • **Cooking time: 1 hour 30 minutes** • **Makes 6 servings** • **Calories: 585, Carbs: 73g, Protein: 49g, Fat: 11g**

Manicotti is a little more trouble than some dishes, but it is well worth the effort and leftovers freeze well.

 1 pound (453g) lean ground round

 3 cloves garlic, minced

 2 onions, chopped

 1 28-ounce (793g) can diced tomatoes, undrained

 1 8-ounce (226g) package fresh mushrooms, sliced

 1 teaspoon fennel seed

 2 teaspoons basil

 1 teaspoon seasoned salt

 1/2 teaspoon pepper

 2 10-ounce (283g) packages frozen chopped spinach, thawed and well drained

 1/2 cup (40g) parmesan cheese, divided

 2 cups (480g) small-curd cottage cheese, drained

 1/4 teaspoon nutmeg

 1/2 teaspoon pepper

 14 manicotti shells, cooked al dente

In a large skillet, brown ground beef, then add garlic and onions, and reduce heat to low. Simmer for 10 minutes and drain. Add tomatoes and liquid, mushrooms, fennel seed, basil, salt, and pepper, and stir to mix. Bring to a boil, reduce heat, and simmer for 10 minutes; stir occasionally.

In a separate bowl, stir together spinach, half the parmesan, cottage cheese, nutmeg, and pepper. In a sprayed 9- x 13-inch (23 x 33 cm) baking dish, spoon about one-third of beef sauce evenly over bottom of dish.

Fill uncooked manicotti shells with spinach mixture and place on beef layer in baking dish. Repeat until all spinach mixture has been used in manicotti shells.

Pour remaining beef sauce evenly over manicotti shells to cover. Sprinkle remaining parmesan cheese over top. Cover and bake at 350° (175° C) for 1 hour 30 minutes or until shells are tender.

Vegetable Roast with Pasta

Prep time: 15 minutes • **Cooking time: 45–50 minutes** • **Makes 6 servings** • **Calories: 371, Carbs: 35g, Protein: 17g, Fat: 19g**

This delicious medley of vegetables and pasta is fit for a king!

3 tablespoons olive oil

2 tablespoons red wine vinegar

3 teaspoons Italian seasoning

½ teaspoon salt

½ teaspoon pepper

2 zucchini, cut in bite-sized pieces

½ pound (226g) fresh mushrooms, halved

1 bunch green onions and tops, cut in 1-inch (2.5 cm) pieces

1 red bell pepper, seeded, cored, cut in bite-sized pieces

1 green bell pepper, seeded, cored, cut in bite-sized pieces

⅓ cup (20g) chopped fresh basil

2 cups (200g) penne pasta

2 tomatoes, seeded, cut into bite-sized pieces

1 8-ounce (226g) package shredded four-cheese blend

In small ovenproof dish, mix together oil, vinegar, Italian seasoning, salt, and pepper. Set aside.

Place zucchini, mushrooms, onions, and bell peppers in sprayed 9- x 13-inch (23 x 33 cm) baking dish and sprinkle top with fresh basil. Drizzle oil and vinegar mixture over top and bake at 350° (175° C) for 35 minutes.

Fill large pot with water and cook penne until al dente. Add tomatoes and pasta to vegetable mixture. Toss to coat, then sprinkle top with cheeses. Bake at 350° (175° C) for 10 to 15 minutes until cheeses are melted.

Southwestern Risotto

Prep time: 20 minutes • **Cooking time: 15–20 minutes** • **Makes 4 to 6 servings** • **Calories: 601, Carbs: 46g, Protein: 13g, Fat: 36g**

Here is a change of pace, and delicious too!

¼ cup (60 mL) olive oil

1 bunch green onions and tops, chopped

½ cup chopped celery

½ cup (85g) chopped red bell pepper

½ cup (85g) chopped green bell pepper

½ cup (85g) chopped yellow bell pepper

1½ cups (335g) uncooked arborio rice

½ cup (120 mL) tequila

2 cups (600 mL) chicken broth

1 16-ounce (453g) package frozen whole kernel corn, thawed

1 8-ounce (226g) package cream cheese

In a large skillet, heat oil and sauté onions, celery, and bell peppers until vegetables are tender. Push vegetables to outside edges of skillet, turn up heat, and add rice to the center.

Toast the rice, toss, and stir until rice grains look translucent. Add tequila and cook until tequila has evaporated and been absorbed. Pour chicken broth into rice ½ cup at a time, and cook until liquid is absorbed. Add corn and stir into rice.

Drop a few cubes of cream cheese into rice, stiring as cheese melts and combines with rice. Continue to add remaining cream cheese and coat all rice with melted cheese.

Serve immediately or pour into a sprayed casserole dish, cool, and refrigerate. To serve, reheat at 350° (175° C) for 15 to 20 minutes or until heated throughout.

Confetti Couscous

Prep time: 10 minutes • **Cooking time: 15 minutes** • **Makes 4 to 6 servings** • **Calories: 705, Carbs: 109g, Protein: 22g, Fat: 20g**

For a change of pace, forget rice or potatoes and lighten up dinner with this delightful, colorful dish.

½ cup (90g) chopped crooknecked or yellow squash

½ cup (90g) chopped zucchini

½ bunch green onions with tops, chopped

¼ cup (25g) chopped celery

¼ cup (45g) chopped red bell pepper

2 cloves garlic, minced

3 tablespoons olive oil

1 14-ounce (396g) can garbanzos, drained

¼ teaspoon cayenne

½ teaspoon cumin

½ teaspoon curry powder

½ teaspoon salt

¼ teaspoon pepper

3 cups (750g) cooked couscous

3 tablespoons butter, melted

Minced green onions or fresh parsley

Sauté over low heat squash, zucchini, onions, celery, bell pepper, and garlic in oil until tender. Stir in garbanzos and seasonings and simmer to mix flavors, for several minutes.

Add couscous and stir to mix. Continue to simmer while stirring to mix. Pour into sprayed baking dish and drizzle butter over top. Bake at 350° (175° C) for 15 minutes until hot. Garnish with minced green onions or fresh parsley.

Herbed Wild Rice Stuffing

Prep time: 15 minutes • **Cooking time: 20–25 minutes** • **Makes 4 to 6 servings** • **Calories: 432, Carbs: 23g, Protein: 15g, Fat: 22g**

Here's a new twist on an old favorite. This stuffing will soon become a family tradition, and can be served with chicken, turkey, pork, or beef.

3 to 4 tablespoons butter

1 cup (100g) chopped celery

1 cup (150g) chopped green onions and tops

2 cloves garlic, minced

3 tablespoons dry white wine

2 tablespoons maple syrup

1 teaspoon sage

1 teaspoon salt

1/2 teaspoon tarragon

1/2 teaspoon poultry seasoning

1/2 teaspoon thyme

3/4 cup (190g) cooked wild rice

8 cups (720g) plain, dry bread cubes

1/2 cup (85g) dried cranberries

1/2 to 1 cup (120 to 240 mL) chicken stock

3 tablespoons chopped fresh parsley

1/2 teaspoon black pepper

In large skillet, melt butter and sauté celery, onion, and garlic until onion is translucent. Add wine, bring to a boil, reduce heat, and simmer for several minutes.

Stir in maple syrup, sage, salt, tarragon, poultry seasoning, and thyme, and mix well. Taste to see if salt is needed.

In a separate bowl, combine wild rice, bread cubes, and cranberries, and toss to mix well. Add onion mixture and stir. Slowly pour in small amount of chicken stock and stir. Mixture should be moist and soupy. (It will dry as it cooks.) Stir in parsley and pepper.

Pour into a sprayed baking dish and bake at 350° (175° C) for 20 to 25 minutes or until heated throughout and golden brown on top.

Cheesy Zucchini Frittata

Prep time: 5 minutes • **Cooking time: 30 minutes** • **Makes 6 servings** • **Calories: 343, Carbs: 23g, Protein: 15g, Fat: 22g**

Although frittatas are famous for their savory herbs and spices, the zucchini and carrots in this recipe add a flavor of their own.

4	eggs
4	cups (700g) shredded zucchini
2	cups (900g) peeled, shredded carrots
1/2	cup (70g) flour
3/4	cup (180g) mayonnaise
1	cup (110g) shredded Monterey Jack cheese
1/2	cup (40g) grated parmesan cheese
1/4	cup (40g) chopped onion
1	teaspoon basil
	Pepper to taste

In mixing bowl beat eggs. Fold in zucchini, carrots, flour, mayonnaise, cheeses, onion, basil, and pepper.

Pour into a buttered quiche pan and bake at 375° (190° C) for 30 minutes or until set.

Apple-Sausage Breakfast Casserole

Prep time: 10 minutes (refrigerate overnight) • **Cooking time: 1 hour** • **Makes 6 servings** • **Calories: 1,012, Carbs: 30g, Protein: 40g, Fat: 81g**

Because this casserole needs to sit overnight before baking, you can sleep in and have a fabulous breakfast, too. Before cooking in the morning, let casserole stand out of refrigerator for 20 to 25 minutes and cook an extra 5 minutes. Delicious served with hot biscuits!

2	pounds (907g) ground pork sausage
8	slices bread
1 1/2	cups (265g) sliced apples
2/3	teaspoons dry mustard
8	eggs, lightly beaten
1 1/2	cups (165g) grated sharp cheddar cheese
3	cups (720 mL) milk

In a large skillet, fry the sausage, breaking it into small bits as it cooks. Drain on paper towels, reserving some of the fat. Lightly grease a 9- x 13-inch (23 x 33 cm) baking dish. Place the sausage in the baking dish.

Remove the crusts from the bread and tear into small pieces or cut into cubes. Sauté the apples in the sausage fat. In a large bowl combine the apples, bread, mustard, eggs, cheese, and milk until well mixed.

Pour the apple mixture over the sausage. Cover with foil and refrigerate overnight. In the morning, bake covered at 350° (175° C) for 30 minutes. Remove the foil and bake uncovered for an additional 30 minutes.

Yellow Squash and Sausage Mix

Prep time: 15 minutes • **Cooking time: 45 minutes** • **Makes 8 servings** • **Calories: 290, Carbs: 12g, Protein: 14g, Fat: 21g**

Summer gardens produce the most beautiful squash! When buying yellow squash, choose the smallest ones since they have fewer seeds.

2 pounds (907g) yellow squash, cut into bite-sized pieces

¼ cup (35g) chopped onion

1 pound (453g) Italian sausage

½ cup (85g) fine cracker crumbs

2 eggs, beaten

½ cup (40g) grated parmesan cheese, divided

¼ teaspoon thyme

¼ teaspoon rosemary

¼ teaspoon garlic powder

Salt and pepper to taste

Cook squash in boiling, salted water until tender; drain. In skillet, brown onion and sausage; drain.

Add squash and remaining ingredients, except 2 tablespoons parmesan cheese, mixing well.

Divide mixture between 2 8-inch (20 cm) pie plates. Sprinkle with remaining parmesan cheese. Bake at 350° (175° C) for 45 minutes, or until brown.

Eggs Mornay

Prep time: 35 minutes • **Cooking time: 25-30 minutes** • **Makes 6 servings** • **Calories: 617, Carbs: 31g, Protein: 26g, Fat: 43g**

Dare to be different: forget the quiche, and serve eggs mornay for lunch or supper. You will get rave reviews!

12	eggs
3	cups (720 mL) milk, divided
1/2	cup (115g) melted butter
1 1/2	teaspoon salt
1/2	teaspoon white pepper
1/4	teaspoon cayenne
1/2	cup (70g) flour
1/2	cup (55g) grated Swiss cheese
1/4	cup (20g) parmesan cheese, divided
1/2	pound (226g) fresh mushrooms, minced
6	tablespoons melted butter, divided
3	tablespoons snipped parsley
1/2	tablespoon snipped tarragon leaves
1	cup (90g) seasoned breadcrumbs
	toast points
	Roma tomatoes, sliced

Carefully place eggs in boiling water and cook until hard-boiled, about 12 to 15 minutes. Remove from heat, drain, and let cool.

Heat milk in large saucepan over low heat until steaming. Pour 2 cups hot milk into blender and set aside remaining hot milk. To blender add butter, salt, white pepper, cayenne, and flour, and blend for 30 seconds.

Pour blender mixture into saucepan with remaining milk and cook over low heat, stirring constantly, until thickened, about 2 to 3 minutes. Add Swiss cheese and half the parmesan cheese to milk and stir until cheese has melted. Remove from heat, cover, and set aside.

Peel shells from eggs and cut lengthwise in half. Separate yolks from whites and set aside. In skillet, sauté mushrooms in 4 tablespoons butter until tender and translucent. Stir in parsley and tarragon.

In a separate bowl, mash egg yolks and stir in 1/2 cup milk-cheese sauce and sautéed mushrooms. Scoop yolk mixture into whites of eggs and set aside.

In a sprayed 9- x 13-inch (23 x 33 cm) baking dish, pour a thin layer of milk-cheese sauce over bottom. Place eggs in baking dish with filling side up. Pour remaining milk-cheese sauce over them.

Toss breadcrumbs with remaining butter and remaining parmesan cheese and sprinkle over eggs. Cover with foil and bake at 350° (175° C) for 25 to 30 minutes. Serve over toast points with fresh sliced tomatoes on the side.

Southern Cheese Grits

Prep time: 10 minutes • **Cooking time: 15–20 minutes** • **Makes 4 servings** • **Calories: 785, Carbs: 17g, Protein: 29g, Fat: 68g**

You haven't experienced breakfast in New Orleans if you haven't had grits served with your eggs!

1 1/2   cups (360 mL) milk

3 1/2   cups (840 mL) water

  1/2   teaspoon salt

1 1/4   cup (190g) quick grits

  1/2   cup (115g) butter

    1   6-ounce (170g) roll garlic cheese

    3   cups (330g) shredded cheddar or colby cheese

  1/2   teaspoon cayenne

  1/2   teaspoon garlic salt

    1   tablespoon Worcestershire sauce

        Paprika

Boil milk, water, and salt in medium saucepan. Add grits and stir to mix. Reduce heat and cook until desired doneness. (Make sure heat is low enough so grits don't stick to bottom of pan.) Stir several times.

Add butter and cheeses and stir to melt. Add cayenne, garlic salt, and Worcestershire sauce. Stir well.

Pour into sprayed 3-quart (3 L) casserole and sprinkle with paprika. Bake covered at 350° (175° C) for 15 to 20 minutes or until thoroughly heated.

Sunrise Baked Potatoes

Prep time: 20 minutes • **Cooking time: 1 hour 45 minutes** • **Makes 4 servings** • **Calories: 588, Carbs: 55g, Protein: 15g, Fat: 35g**

Perk up any meal with these "twice baked" potatoes! (To speed up the cooking process, push metal skewers through centers to conduct heat.)

4	Idaho baking potatoes
	Olive oil or butter
1/2	pound (226g) hot, ground pork sausage
1	cup (150g) chopped green onion with tops, divided
1/4	cup (45g) minced red bell pepper
1/4	cup (60 mL) whipping cream
3	egg yolks
1/4	cup (60g) sour cream
1	teaspoon salt
1/2	teaspoon white pepper
	Hungarian paprika
	Fresh parsley
	Fresh tomato slices

Wash potatoes and stick skins several times with fork. Rub skins with a little oil or butter and arrange on baking sheet. Bake at 350° (175° C) for 1 hour 30 minutes or until potatoes are soft on the inside. Remove potatoes from oven to cool.

Brown sausage in skillet until crumbly and cooked through. Drain sausage on paper towels and transfer to large mixing bowl. Add a little oil to skillet, and sauté 3/4 cup green onion and red bell pepper until tender and translucent. Add onion and bell pepper to sausage in mixing bowl.

When potatoes are cool enough to touch, cut small ovals in outer skin on top of potatoes. With a small spoon, scoop out pulp, being careful to leave shell intact. Leave about 1/4-inch (6 mm) thickness inside outer skin.

Put potato pulp in a separate bowl and mash with a fork or potato masher. Slowly stir in whipping cream, egg yolks, sour cream, salt, and white pepper. Stir well to mix ingredients and to make a creamy texture. Add a little more cream if mixture seems too dry.

Slowly fold in sausage-onion mixture and stir to combine. Spoon this filling into individual potato shells, allowing filling to rise above top of potato skin. Place stuffed potatoes back on baking sheet and sprinkle top of each potato with paprika.

Bake at 350° (175° C) for 10 to 15 minutes to heat thoroughly. Remove from oven and garnish with parsley and remaining minced green onion tops. Serve with tomato slices on the side.

Spinach Quiche

Prep time: 15 minutes • **Cooking time: 30–45 minutes** • **Makes 6 servings** • **Calories: 421, Carbs: 16g, Protein: 15g, Fat: 34g**

This is a great dish to serve at a luncheon. You will want to make this quiche lots of times, so invest in a metal quiche pan that has a removable bottom.

1	10-ounce (283g) package frozen chopped spinach
1	9-inch (23 cm) pastry shell
1/4	cup (20g) grated parmesan cheese
3	eggs, beaten
1 1/2	cups (337g) cottage cheese, drained
1	cup (240 mL) whipping cream
2	tablespoons minced onion
1 1/2	teaspoons salt
1/2	teaspoon pepper
1	teaspoon caraway seeds
1/4	teaspoon nutmeg
1/2	teaspoon Worcestershire sauce
3	drops Tabasco sauce
3	tablespoons butter, melted

Cook spinach according to package directions and drain thoroughly. Line the pie pan with pastry and bake at 400° (200° C) for 8 minutes. Remove from oven and cool. Reduce oven temperature to 350° (175° C).

Sprinkle parmesan cheese in bottom of shell. Combine all remaining ingredients except butter. Pour butter over cheese. Melt butter and pour over top.

Bake for 30 to 45 minutes or until toothpick comes out clean.

Southern Carrot-Pecan Casserole

Prep time: 30 minutes • Cooking time: 45 minutes • Makes 8 servings • Calories: 293, Carbs: 38g, Protein: 5g, Fat: 15g

This is not your average carrot casserole: This dish could easily be put in the gourmet category of carrots for the "discriminating" palate!

- 3   pounds (1.4 kg) carrots, peeled and sliced
- 4   tablespoons butter, softened
- 2/3   cups (140g) sugar
- 2/3   cups (70g) chopped pecans, toasted
- 1/4   cups (60 mL) milk
- 2   eggs, slightly beaten
- 3   tablespoons flour
- 1 1/4 teaspoon vanilla extract
- 1 1/2 tablespoon grated orange rind
- 1/4   teaspoon ground nutmeg

In saucepan, cover carrots with water and boil 15 to 20 minutes, just until tender. Spread pecans over baking sheet in one layer. Bake at 250° (120° C) for 10 to 15 minutes, stirring once or twice. Remove from oven to cool.

Drain carrots and mash. Blend in butter, sugar, pecans, and remaining ingredients until thoroughly mixed. Spoon into a lightly greased, 8-inch (20 cm) baking dish. Bake at 350° (175° C) for 45 minutes.

Cheesy Asparagus

Prep time: 5 minutes • **Cooking time: 20–25 minutes** • **Makes 4 servings** • **Calories: 606, Carbs: 46g, Protein: 27g, Fat: 37g**

Asparagus is often reserved as a special dish for company, but your family will also ask for this casserole on a regular basis.

2 15-ounce (400g) cans asparagus spears, liquid reserved

1/2 stick (120g) butter

5 tablespoons flour

Salt and pepper to taste

1/2 cup (120 mL) milk

1/2 teaspoon Worcestershire sauce

Dash cayenne pepper

4 eggs, boiled, sliced

1/4 pound (113g) cheddar cheese, cubed

1/2 cup (40g) almonds, sliced

1 cup (175g) crushed Ritz Cracker crumbs

Reserve 3/4 cup (180 mL) asparagus liquid and set asparagus aside. In saucepan melt the butter and gradually blend in flour until smooth, adding salt and pepper.

Slowly add asparagus liquid and milk, stirring until thickened and smooth. You may add more milk if liquid is too thick. Add Worcestershire sauce and cayenne pepper.

Layer the casserole in an 8- x 11-inch (20 x 28 cm) baking pan as follows: asparagus, eggs, cheese, and almonds, and repeat layers. Spoon sauce over layers. Sprinkle cracker crumbs over casserole and bake at 350° (175° C) for 20 to 25 minutes.

Broccoli Casserole Amandine

Prep time: 10 minutes • Cooking time: 20 minutes • Makes 4 servings • Calories: 522, Carbs: 24g, Protein: 22g, Fat: 40g

President Bush (senior) is the only person in the world who doesn't like broccoli—and it is so healthy, (just don't tell the kids).

- 2 10-ounce (283g) packages frozen chopped broccoli
- 3 tablespoons butter
- 2 tablespoons flour
- 2 cups (480 mL) milk
- 3/4 cup (60g) grated parmesan
- 1 teaspoon salt
- 1/4 teaspoon ground pepper
- 1/4 pound (113g) mushrooms, sliced
- 1/2 cup (40g) chopped almonds
- 4 slices cooked bacon, crumbled
- 1/2 cup (90g) buttered breadcrumbs
  Dash paprika

Cook broccoli according to package directions; drain. Place broccoli in a sprayed baking dish.

In a saucepan, melt butter and blend in flour. Add milk and cook until thick, stirring constantly. Add cheese and stir until melted. Season with salt and pepper and add mushrooms.

Remove from heat and pour sauce into a sprayed 2-quart (2 L) baking dish. Put almonds and bacon on top of broccoli. Sprinkle with breadcrumbs and paprika. Bake at 350° (175° C) for 20 minutes.

Squash Tomato Bake

Prep time: 20 minutes • **Cooking time: 25–30 minutes** • **Makes 4 servings** • **Calories: 274, Carbs: 25g, Protein: 21g, Fat: 12g**

You can't beat this combination of squash, tomato, and mozzarella cheese.

1 pound (453g) zucchini, sliced

1 pound (453g) yellow squash, sliced

2 15-ounce (425g) cans Italian stewed tomatoes

2 teaspoons sugar

2 tablespoons flour

1 teaspoon paprika

1 teaspoon salt

1/4 teaspoon white pepper

1/2 teaspoon basil

1/4 teaspoon garlic powder

2 cups (220g) shredded mozzarella cheese, divided

1/3 cup (30g) grated parmesan cheese

Cook squash in saucepan, almost covered in water . Bring water to a boil, reduce heat, and simmer for 5 to 10 minutes, stirring several times, until squash is fork tender. Drain and set aside.

In a saucepan, pour 1/2 cup of liquid from the tomatoes and mix with sugar, flour, paprika, salt, pepper, basil, and garlic powder. Heat for 5 to 10 minutes, stirring several times, and remove from heat.

In a sprayed 2-quart (2 L) baking dish, layer half the squash, one-third of the tomato mixture, half the mozzarella, and one-third of the tomato mixture.

Repeat all layers with remaining squash, tomato mixture, and mozzarella. Bake at 350° (175° C) for 20 to 25 minutes. Remove from oven, sprinkle parmesan over top, and return to oven, covered, for 5 minutes. Let stand for 10 minutes before serving.

Arugula Mashed Potatoes

Prep time: 30–40 minutes • **Cooking time: 25–30 minutes** • **Makes 6 servings** • **Calories: 392, Carbs: 46g, Protein: 10g, Fat: 19g**

Try a different taste for a mashed potato favorite.

3 to 4 cloves garlic

¼ cup (60 mL) olive oil, divided

Salt

White pepper

3 pounds (1.4 kg) baking potatoes

2 14-ounce (414 mL) cans chicken broth

2 bunches arugula, washed

4 tablespoons butter, divided

2 cups (480 mL) milk, divided

Fresh parsley

Fresh green onions with tops

Paprika

Place garlic cloves on aluminum foil. Coat with small amount olive oil and sprinkle with salt and pepper. Loosely close foil. Place in small baking dish and bake at 350° (175° C) for 30 to 40 minutes until garlic is soft. Remove from oven to cool. Set aside.

Wash potatoes thoroughly and peel them. (It's acceptable to leave peels on the potatoes, as many people prefer.) Cut them into large chunks, put in large saucepan, and cover with chicken broth and water. Bring broth to boil, reduce heat slightly, and cook for 25 to 30 minutes until potatoes are soft.

Wash arugula thoroughly to remove all grit from leaves. Hold bottom of arugula with tongs, and dip the leaves into boiling broth of potatoes. Drain on power towels, pull leaves apart, and pat dry. Snip larger leaves into smaller pieces and set aside.

When potatoes are soft enough to mash with a fork, drain and remove from saucepan. Empty water from pan and return pan to heat for a few seconds just to dry out all the water.

Remove pan from heat and add potatoes. Mash with fork until all lumps are gone. Squeeze roasted garlic from outer skins and mash on separate plate. Add garlic and half the butter to potatoes, and stir to mix. Continue mashing to remove all lumps.

Slowly pour milk into potatoes, stirring constantly. Use the amount of milk necessary for the consistency of mashed potatoes you want: more milk for creamy, less milk for drier.

Drizzle potatoes with olive oil, and add salt and white pepper generously. Add half the arugula and taste. Adjust salt, pepper, and butter, and add more arugula to taste. Garnish with any remaining arugula, parsley, or green onions with tops. Sprinkle with paprika, if desired.